Skateboarding Greats:
Champs of the Ramps

By Angie Peterson Kaelberer

Content Consultant:
Pete Connelly
Staff writer, *Heckler* magazine

CAPSTONE
HIGH-INTEREST
BOOKS

an imprint of Capstone Press
Mankato, Minnesota

Capstone High-Interest Books are published by Capstone Press
151 Good Counsel Drive, P.O. Box 669, Mankato, Minnesota 56002
http://www.capstone-press.com

Library of Congress Cataloging-in-Publication Data
Kaelberer, Angie Peterson.
    Skateboarding greats: champs of the ramps/by Angie Peterson Kaelberer.
    p. cm.—(Skateboarding)
    Includes bibliographical references and index.
    Summary: Describes the top skateboarders throughout the history of the
sport, from those of the 1970s to the top performers of the early 2000s.
    ISBN 0-7368-1074-9
    1. Skateboarders—United States—Biography—Juvenile literature.
[1. Skateboarders. 2. Skateboarding—History.] I. Title. II. Series.
GV859.8 .K34 2002
796.22'092'2—dc21   2001003924

Editorial Credits
Timothy Halldin, cover designer, interior layout designer, and interior
    illustrator; Katy Kudela, photo researcher

Photo Credits
Glen E. Friedman, 8, 11, 12
Gunter Marx Photography/CORBIS, 14
Isaac Hernandez/Mercury Press International, 4, 6, 7 (all), 29
Jed Jacobsohn/ALLSPORT PHOTOGRAPHY, 24
M. David Leeds/ALLSPORT PHOTOGRAPHY, cover, 23
Patrick Batchelder, 20
SportsChrome-USA/Rob Tringali Jr., 26
Vandystadt/ALLSPORT PHOTOGRAPHY, 17, 18

1 2 3 4 5 6 07 06 05 04 03 02

Table of Contents

Tony Hawk prepared to do a 900 at the 1999 X Games.

CHAPTER ONE

From Amateur to Professional

On June 27, 1999, more than 8,000 skateboarding fans gathered at the X Games in San Francisco, California. The fans were there to watch professional skater Tony Hawk compete in the Best Trick competition.

The fans hoped to see Hawk complete a 900. During this trick, a skater rides up a ramp and spins two and one-half times in the air before landing. No skater had ever completed this trick in competition.

Learn About

- Tony Hawk's 900
- Amateurs and professionals
- Skating teams

Hawk celebrated after he completed the 900.

The 900

Hawk made 10 attempts to complete the 900. Each time, he fell.

Hawk built his speed by skating twice up and down the ramp. He then took off from the top of the ramp. He spun two and one-half times in the air before landing on his board.

The crowd cheered as other skaters lifted him into the air.

Amateurs and Professionals

The first skateboarding competition took place in 1963 in Hermosa, California. This contest was an amateur competition. The skaters did not earn prize money for competing. Most professional skaters begin their careers as amateurs. They develop their skills before turning professional.

Professional skaters have sponsors. These companies pay for the skater's equipment and traveling expenses. Most skateboarding equipment companies sponsor a team of skaters. Skaters on these teams travel together and compete at the same events.

Skater Tony Alva grew up in Santa Monica.

CHAPTER TWO

Early Greats

Many of the first skateboarders were surfers. Surfers thought that skateboarding was like surfing on land. They liked the speed and feeling of freedom that skateboarding gave them.

In the 1970s, many of the world's top skaters lived in or near Santa Monica, California. This city has many empty swimming pools and other concrete surfaces that attract skaters.

Learn About

- Tony Alva
- Stacy Peralta
- Alan Gelfand

Tony Alva

Tony Alva was born in 1957 in Santa Monica. He began skating at age 10.

Alva also surfed. He brought his surfing style into his skating. Alva liked to skate in empty pools. Alva also skated in large concrete pipes found in drainage ditches and at construction sites. Today's half-pipe ramps are based on these pipes. These ramps also are called vert ramps. Skaters who perform on these ramps are called vert skaters.

By 1975, Alva was a member of the Zephyr surfboard company's skating team. This team was called the Z-Boys. In 1976, he won the Men's Overall World Professional Skateboard Championship.

Stacy Peralta

Stacy Peralta was born in 1959 in Santa Monica. He began skating at age 6. By age 16, he was a member of the Z-Boys.

In 1978, Powell Skateboards asked Peralta to help the company form a skating team. The team's

Stacy Peralta helped form the Bones Brigade skating team.

official name was Powell Peralta. But people called the team the "Bones Brigade." The name comes from the white wheels on Powell skateboards. The company called the wheels "bones."

In 1991, Peralta left the Powell company. In 2001, he wrote and directed a movie about Santa Monica skaters. The movie is called *Dogtown and Z-Boys.*

Alan Gelfand

Alan Gelfand was born in 1963 in New York. He grew up in Hollywood, Florida. In 1978, Gelfand invented a new skateboarding trick in a skatepark pool. Gelfand stepped hard on the board's tail. This action made the nose pop up. Gelfand rose into the air and landed back on the board. Gelfand then learned to do his trick on a ramp. He could make the board pop 2 feet (.6 meter) into the air.

Gelfand's friends called him "Ollie." They called his new trick an "ollie pop." Other skaters soon shortened the trick's name to the ollie. Today, most skateboarding tricks begin with an ollie.

In 1979, Gelfand joined the Bones Brigade. He spent the next two years traveling the world with the team. He retired from professional skating in 1981.

Alan Gelfand invented the ollie.

Skateboarding again became popular in the mid-1980s.

CHAPTER THREE

The 1980s

The early 1980s were not good years for skateboarding. Most skateparks closed. Many people lost interest in the sport.

But skateboarding remained popular in warmer areas of the United States. These areas included California and Florida. By the mid-1980s, skateboarding had become popular again throughout North America. The sport had a new group of stars.

Learn About

- Rodney Mullen
- Steve Caballero
- Mike McGill

15

Steve Caballero

Steve Caballero was born in 1964. He grew up in Campbell, California. He started skating at age 12. At 14, he joined the Bones Brigade.

Caballero became one of the top street skaters in the 1980s. Street skaters perform tricks on objects located on city streets. These objects include curbs and stairway handrails.

Caballero also invented the Caballerial. This trick is a fakie 360 ollie. To do this trick, a skater begins the ollie in a fakie or backward position. The skater then spins a full circle in the air before landing on the board.

Rodney Mullen

In the 1980s, people called Rodney Mullen "the king of freestyle." Freestyle skaters usually skate on flat surfaces such as parking lots.

Mullen was born in 1966 in Gainesville, Florida. He began skating at age 10. In 1980, he joined the

Steve Caballero was a top street skater in the 1980s.

Bones Brigade. He won nearly every freestyle contest that he entered.

In the 1990s, freestyle skating became less popular. Mullen then began street skating. He combined freestyle moves with street moves to create his own skating style.

Mike McGill was a top vert skater in the 1970s and 1980s.

Skateboarding videos became popular by the mid-1980s. Many of these videos included members of professional skating teams. *Bones Brigade* and *SKATE VISIONS* were two popular early videos.

Mike McGill

Mike McGill was born in Florida in 1964. He began skating at age 11. By age 15, he was winning contests in California and Florida.

McGill turned professional in 1982. He skated for the Bones Brigade.

In 1984, McGill invented the 540 McTwist. This trick combines a twist with a 540-degree spin.

In 1986, McGill opened his own skatepark in Carlsbad, California. He retired from professional skating in the late 1980s.

The X Games began in 1995.

Today's Greats

In 1995, the ESPN TV network started a new extreme sports competition. This competition was called the Extreme Games. Later, ESPN changed the competition's name to the X Games. The competition includes skateboarding. Many people watched the X Games and became interested in skateboarding.

Learn About

- Tony Hawk
- Andy Macdonald
- Bob Burnquist

Tony Hawk

Tony Hawk is one of the best and most well-known of today's skaters. His career has lasted more than 20 years.

Hawk was born in 1968 in San Diego, California. He began skating at age 9 and turned professional at 14. He joined the Bones Brigade in 1981. He skated for the team until 1991.

Hawk was the top vert skater during the 1990s. He competed in more than 100 competitions and placed first in more than 70. This record is the best in pro skateboarding. He won the gold medal in vert at the 1995 and 1997 X Games.

Hawk invented more than 80 skateboarding tricks. He was the first skater to perform the 720 and the 900 in competition. A skater makes two complete spins in the air during a 720.

Tony Hawk's skateboard company is called Birdhouse Projects.

Today, Hawk does not often compete in singles skating events. But he still competes in doubles events. Two skaters compete together during these events. Hawk also owns a skateboard company. The company is called Birdhouse Projects. Hawk has helped design two skateboarding video games. In 2000, he wrote a book about his life. The book is called *HAWK: Occupation: Skateboarder.*

Andy Macdonald

Andy Macdonald was born in 1973 in Boston, Massachusetts. He began skating at age 12. He turned professional in 1994.

Macdonald competes in both vert and street competitions. He was the World Cup Skateboarding overall combined champion from 1996 to 2000. He won the gold medal in vert at the 1996 and 1998 X Games. He also won the vert gold medal at the 2000 Gravity Games.

Macdonald teams with Tony Hawk to skate in vert doubles events. Hawk and Macdonald won gold medals in vert doubles at each X Games from 1997 to 2001.

Andy Macdonald competes in street and vert events.

Bob Burnquist won the Best Trick competition at the 2000 X Games.

Bob Burnquist is one of the first modern skaters to skate switchstance in competition. His normal skating stance is regular. He skates with his left foot in front. But he also can skate goofy foot. Goofy-foot skaters have their right foot in front.

Bob Burnquist

Bob Burnquist was born in 1976 in Rio de Janeiro, Brazil. His father is from the United States and his mother is from Brazil. He grew up in São Paulo, Brazil.

Burnquist started skating at age 11 on the São Paulo streets. In 1995, he entered and won his first skating competition. This contest was the North American Skateboard Championships in Vancouver, British Columbia, Canada. This competition also is called the Slam City Jam.

Since 1995, Burnquist has won many skating competitions. In 1999, he won the gold medal at the Gravity Games. He won the Best Trick competition at the 2000 X Games. In 2001, he placed first in vert at the X Games.

Women in Skateboarding

Over the years, most of the top skaters have been men. But many women also have done well in the sport.

Ellen Oneal was a top freestyle skater in the 1970s. She was known for performing skateboarding tricks on two boards.

Many people consider Cara-Beth Burnside the top female skater of the 1990s. She began skating in 1986 and turned professional in 1990. Burnside also is a snowboarder. In 1998, she won the gold medal in the snowboard half-pipe competition at the X Games.

Street skater Elissa Steamer and vert skater Jen O'Brien are two of today's top female skaters. Steamer grew up in Fort Myers, Florida. She began skateboarding at age 12. She turned professional in 1998. O'Brien is from Deland, Florida. She started skating at age 16.

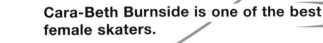

Cara-Beth Burnside is one of the best female skaters.

Words to Know

amateur (AM-uh-chur)—someone who participates in a sport without being paid

Caballerial (kah-buh-LAIR-ee-uhl)—a fakie 360 ollie invented by Steve Caballero

fakie (FAY-kee)—a trick that is performed backward or opposite of the usual position

ollie (AH-lee)—a trick in which the skater steps on the board's tail to make the board rise into the air

professional (pruh-FESH-uh-nuhl)—a person who receives money for taking part in a sport

sponsor (SPON-sur)—a business that helps pay an athlete's expenses; athletes use the sponsor's products in return.

To Learn More

Freimuth, Jeri. *Extreme Skateboarding Moves.* Behind the Moves. Mankato, Minn.: Capstone High-Interest Books, 2001.

Martin, Michael. *History of Skateboarding: From the Backyard to the Big Time.* Skateboarding. Mankato, Minn.: Capstone High-Interest Books, 2002.

Stout, Glenn. *On the Halfpipe with—Tony Hawk.* Boston: Little, Brown, and Company, 2001.

Useful Addresses

ESPN X Games
3524 California Street
San Francisco, CA 94118

Transworld Skateboarding Magazine
353 Airport Road
Oceanside, CA 92054

Internet Sites

EXPN.com
http://expn.go.com

Transworld Skateboarding.com
http://www.skateboarding.com

WCSK8.com 2001
http://www.wcsk8.com

Index